C000005110

HYMN TO THE RECKLESS

First published in 2017 by
The Dedalus Press
13 Moyclare Road
Baldoyle
Dublin D13 K1C2
Ireland

www.**dedaluspress**.com

Copyright © Erin Fornoff, 2017

ISBN 978 1 910251 26 3

All rights reserved.
No part of this publication may be reproduced in any form
or by any means without the prior permission
of the publisher.

The moral right of the author has been asserted.

Dedalus Press titles are represented in the UK by
Inpress Books, www.inpressbooks.co.uk,
and in North America by Syracuse University Press, Inc.,
www.syracuseuniversitypress.syr.edu.

Erin Fornoff can be found online at
@jarsofshine and www.erinfornoff.com.

Cover image by kind permission of Bryan Derballa.

The Dedalus Press receives financial assistance from
The Arts Council / An Chomhairle Ealaíon.

HYMN TO THE RECKLESS

ERIN FORNOFF

DEDALUS PRESS

ACKNOWLEDGEMENTS

Acknowledgement is due to the journals and anthologies which have published some of these poems, or versions of them, including *The Stinging Fly, Skylight 47, Icarus, New Planet Cabaret, Waco Word Fest Anthology,* and Stewed Rhubarb Press in its *Folk Heroes* chapbook. 'Throughout' won the 2016 Listowel Originals Short Poem Competition. A video version of 'August in New Orleans' won the Stanza Digital Slam in 2013 and was featured on the Stanza Festival website. 'Hymn to the Reckless' came third in the 2013 Strokestown Poetry Competition and was chosen by Poetry Ireland to feature on posters and cards nationwide and included in the programme for National Poetry Day 2016. A version of 'Unwieldy Pasture' was shortlisted for the Bridport Prize. Some of these poems have been broadcast on radio in the UK, and in Ireland on RTÉ's *Arena* and on Newstalk, and videos have been shared widely online.

The author wishes to thank Listowel Writers Week for offering a 10-day residency at Cill Rialaig, without which this book could not have been completed. Thanks to thoughtful readers and friends whose insight improved both my sanity and these poems: Miranda Richmond Mouillot, Colm Keegan, Elaine Feeney, Dave Tynan, Sarah Clancy, Collier McLeod, Jill Kring, Linda Devlin, Teresa Ginsberg, Claire Hennessy, John Harris, Sarah Griffin, Kalle Ryan and Johnny Taylor and Dave Knox. Bryan Derballa offered the cover photo. Thanks to those who allowed me to read and perform these pieces over the past few years. The Irish poetry community is alive and kicking, and so very precious.

CONTENTS

1

2

3

4

To Dottie and Dave

1

Hymn to the Reckless

for Reed Fornoff, my brother

Together we throw flame into orbit.
The frantic patter, the volley, the hit—
from afar it's just stars come down to flit.

We bend quick to the flame and pull coals into flight,
a delirious slight of hand with a teaspoon of light.
Once one caught between my fingers and seared,
and that night I wrapped my aching hand around cold beer.

We're boozy folk heroes performing incredible feats,
craft exquisite trajectories with arms full of heat.
Look! the arc as he sends it hurtling toward me
bending with some eccentric choreography—

we burn. Our power, to drag a new comet trail across the evening,
a hymn to the reckless, so breathless it falls to earth, the air
    singeing—
we smoulder. Gods of our own solstice, and solace, there's solace
in this insane game; in being the wild ones who manhandle coals
from the flames and make them dance.

Oh! he catches behind the back, he's a one-man eclipse of the sun,
lays cursive lines across your eyelids even once you've closed them.
With a tap-tap-tap it comes flying to me, oh God—I got it!
Lightning quick layup—I shot it, always skyward.

We marvel at our savage skill, at what we've harnessed.
Sleep hard with sooty hands, flames peel off the varnish.

One night in the smoke with his throat full, he turned, stilled,
    confessed:
You know, I always thought they loved you best.

How long has he held that pressed tight in his palm
as it scorched him? Brave in the dim to de-clench that fist
from the ember within; to admit what forges us.
The gentle soul who can cast flame to the rim of the sky.

And the ember. Exposed to air it glows, it catches, it dies, it passes.
Throw it here. We'll toss it back and forth until it's ashes.

Small Town Synaesthesia

At the station, slicks of oil tie-dye the puddles
in the concrete, below the pumps, as they tick over
the litres and gallons. They reflect the sun,
turn it wild, hold it in the cracked dips of the ground.

When he balances the till at the end of the shift
the numbers throb coloured across the spectrum;
they cast a lemon scent when the totals align.

The streetlight haze makes him taste salt.
Sneakers hum, make a pale green sound
as players fight for the rebound.

Colour: his secret language. Smell and taste and noise:
his tangled fluency. Can he grow to see his unruly filter
as a gift, beyond affliction? Turn his own faulty wiring
into some exalted circuitry?

The door chimes in the town's one restaurant.
It blooms a purple sheen behind his eyes and dims
as the noise fades. They know him when he walks in.

He's been hanging out at this same gas station,
drinking this same beer, having this same chat,
since growing pains dishevelled his sleep. He's mastered
the edit of his own thoughts.

Small towns remake teenagers
into polished stones, tumbled by peer pressure,
grey as concrete. Every sound dances an acid trip
across his brain. He wonders what shapes

the train whistle makes when it blows
in other places. He is oil catching sunlight.

Tree House

The beech is all soar and space,
skin like an elephant, smooth as bed sheets.
It is the erasing of a tree among the pines' feral
cross-hatch, their crusts of bark.

Its arching grace caught us. We hauled boards
and nails as our morning bloomed plans.
Look at a beech long enough, you want
to run your hands up its trunk like a lover.

We laid over the crotch of its branches
a tongue-and-groove floor, a forest parquet
open to the sky, smooth enough to lay a cheek on.
Hammered low walls beneath the canopy and clouds.

But a ballroom floor proves unfit for the elements.
Slowly black leaves clumped. The clouds brought rain.
Rain brought mould. The trunk pushed outward as it thickened.

The whole operation crumpled, a receipt in a fist,
as the tree opened skyward and spread.
We had welcomed the weather, chosen no roof, denied
the inevitability of season and gravity. Grown up.

Swimming in Winter

We were that kind of delicious limp
that comes from being extremely cold
then plunged into warmth,
where all your muscles just sort of
give up in one go, and lay the burden
on your bones to hold you up.
He sat next to me, head back,
looking up at the whooshing night
through the rear windshield,
skeleton trees arcing over the road
like some Victorian conservatory
as we drove back from the river.

We filled two cars halfway through the night,
drove down the switchbacks to the straightway
in Gerton, deep in a cove, leftover snow in pockets
of shadow and ledge. The river roared
and the six of us crept, cursing, to the water's edge.

Quietly we assessed each other's willingness:
one detected pause and we'd call the game and go—
but no. A midnight winter jump into the pool
at the bend in the river, with the soaring rock
cracked halfway down, the collected rush
of cascades as the water poured down the mountain.

In the car, jeans damp, heads wet and melting,
we inhaled each other's warmth. Next to me he
was mostly quiet, now and then threw a joke
over the front seat to the boys.

Something of winter air in the mountains gives
a brisk, almost painful clarity, lines even in the darkness
so clear it stings. Pride, almost a crime,
and the effervescent cold; some bold transgression
pushed our jumping, the screams exaggerated
for the group's behalf, the heaving lung,
the clawing for the rocks again. The exalted cries.
Our groove in memory. Standing in the bare air after:
each of us a column of steam.

Moonshine

Apples ground-scattered as if thrown,
sides gone soft, wormholes like cigarette burns.
We gather them, shake sugar and yeast,
stir until the pulp bubbles in gastric ferment.

We wait for a sunny day and begin early,
haul deep pots and propane up the hill
back where the rain-rubbed mountains meet.
We connect the pipes, and flick a lighter.

The mixture comes alive over the hiss
as we tamp the top down, screw the coil,
run cold creek water over the metal's rising heat.
The steam scatters crawdads and salamander.

We catch the first drips, clear as rainwater,
as the boiling mash breathes alcohol
and the copper pipes release their slow weeping
that burns cold on the fingers, blue in a flame.

And with a sip it sears a line down the oesophagus,
pulls an instinctual cringe, the pursed lip, double chin,
the performance of the exhale, the cuss. The purity of rot.
The life in Appalachian cliché.

What proof comes from this task?
What marvels from decay?
What proof am I, a distiller in the boiling?

The hills flow far away, trees wind-sentient,
as the glass jar fills. We screw the lid.

The horizon lifts across the valley,
and its image refracts and bends
as we hold it to the light.

2

Murmuration

for Conor Walsh

He traced the lines of familiar road,
the half-thought drive west through thick darkness,
a cascade of melody from the blue-lit radio
like some glorious exhalation from the speakers.

It is a devotion pulling like a prayer. Alert,
almost there, he braked to a stop as a stag stood
in his high beams on the two-lane.

Unstartled, it seemed to square itself
in the aquarium glare of the lights;
unapologetic, poised for flight,
poured with an unknowable kindness.

He turned his key halfway, like a decision.
It is bending to the task until the notes breathe.
It is standing before a powerful stillness
and listening.

He opened the door and stepped out
onto the centre line, the tarmac, rough and even,
gripping beneath his feet.

The stag, a still monument, antlers branched
and soaring, did not blink its wet eye. Interrupted
in their crossings, they shared a caught sigh,
notes rising in low murmuration from the stereo.

He breathed. It is choosing to yoke yourself
to what you love. In the charged dark,
moving slow, he reached past the pinging of the door
and turned that floating music up.

Swimming with Seals

You can see she's still a dancer by her stretch
in reaching for a cup on a high shelf, how
she swims as one long sinew from fingertip
to pointed toe; an even stroke past the breakers.

We jump. The cold is a slap that leaves me
clutching at air. It doesn't even faze her.
We're at the bare edge of cliffs that rear up
so high overhead we arch onto our backs
to get their measure.

We can see past Dalkey Island to Portmarnock,
past Greystones' ruined harbor to Wicklow Head,
and two tyre-backed seals arise from nowhere,
heads cocked with questions. I tread water;

she goes out with them farther than I dare,
out to where the current sweeps hard left
towards Dublin Bay and the stream of it
catches the light, the nap of its surface
an oily river through the water.

She works the lines of her body, dives as they dive
and rise. They bob like needles embroidering
as they go below. They are alien
and fluent in the heaving sea.
Their motion translates as a kind of joy.

They always seem to be playing
even in the serious work of survival. Her brown back
weaves with the seals. She laughs

and in the yawn of sea and air it echoes.
The shock of the water snatches my breath.
And this steals whatever breath I had left.

Monk

I saw the toe pads of a monk
had worn into the wood, his daily prayer
a stationary weight that pressed
the whorl like thumbs into clay.

I am an anthropologist of that kind
of devotion:

a life set down like a box
and pushed across the floor
in offering.

Once, I met a man who drove
all across the country, wrappers
accumulated beneath the seats
like leaf-fall,
just to preach the Gospel.

College students, hungover, in constant
nervous assessment, we found him crazy
as he wielded the black book,
as he lifted up his eyes.

He turned his whole body into an instrument
just to play harmony for God.
He rubbed that love with his whole life
until it shone.

It doesn't feel safe to love
that much. To stand and pray
until your feet sink into the floor.

File it under the one dream I can remember

Me now, meets me, then:
she's small, lying on her belly.
the same eyes, squared-off nose,
features a bit too big for our face.
Black-headed like our mother.

She's bent to the paper, fist wrapping a crayon,
engrossed, as usual. She looks up at old me—
5'6", done growing, woman now,
half confidence, half apology.

We gaze at one another,
her settled down there,
at home among sheaves of blank paper.

Standing, I am nearly shy. She looks up,
seems to decide something,
returns to her drawing. I lie
down on the floor beside her.
I take a piece of paper.

Rough Seas

I manufactured a kinship with the sea:
when the surf slid up the beach,
I read it as affection,
as though it shared with me
a mutual nostalgia.

It flirted. It tweaked my ankles.
It matched me: the arch of shore to the curve
of my lumbar spine, my arms child-wide
before its bowed horizon. Its beating waves
a heart. Salty as my blood.

But when I fell over the rocks, pulled
into the moaning boil, it ignored me,
pounded my sinuses, churned:
I found myself an animal whose gifts
of persuasion had no currency.
All I could speak was panic.

My body flailed,
its chemicals frothed,
reached and found nothing to hold—
air like a desperate gift offered and retracted,
offered and retracted—
all of it overlaid by gasp and frenzy—
a slow sense rising: I am all alone.

Between the thrash and spatter,
the suck of the moon, the darkened granite:
I am the thing that breaks.

Confidante

We've had pints
enough between us
to crowd this small table
with their empty columns.
It's late enough
to say what we're thinking
as you do on nights
such as these. I start.
So what's the deal with you and ...
And she says
Don't ask me.
Don't ask me what I know
you're going to ask.
And I understand
I've plunged up to my elbows
in a real messy question,
hauled it dripping
onto the table, left it
splatted among the glasses.
I know how an answer
can define things
or strip them bare
but it still stings
to go un-confided in,
to leave the answer
empty of any weight
and feel guilty for the question.
I want to know
if they went home
I want to know
if she loves him

I want to know
if he calls her
when it suits him.
And I wonder
if the hunger
of my knowing
is why
she doesn't say.

My Three Solaces

for Dave Knox

the solace
of leaving a party

the solace
of a warm place
with a storm
raging

the solace
of the couch
sunk
with your weight

I do not know

if this lifetime's training
can withstand the onslaught.

Politeness as identity is taxing:
niceness bends but doesn't knot,
a pulled branch, released, becomes a whip.

I cannot spend another restaurant meal
grimly eating the wrong order, for another's sake.
Swallowing some demanded compromise.

The table under this plate cries out for flipping.
My mouth dares me: unwrap these teeth from smiling.

Try me.
I do not know if I am sun or storm.

Unwieldy Pasture

for Elaine Collins

The cows clot at the fence gate as though crowding a drain.
She stands, a half-hearted sentinel, on the monthly summons
for extra hands. Wellies pull at her thighs, the lurching roll
of slow eyes, the heat, the dull ground shake when they come.

A blunt spark in consciousness amid the momentum
releases panic smelled like smoke, unfurls an urgent flight,
a lolling run, heavy mass pounding, and her father
is overtaken at the fence gate. She sees him fall.

She sees him stay down. She flings her heavy legs
and runs to him. He could rise—is arising—but has shifted
somehow, and the moment is like a gasp she can not exhale.

It fills her with his impermanence until her lungs could burst.
She smudges away the jagged filigree of worry
by taking the piss—*you feckin eejit*—but her ribs separate
and float over the knowledge in that air.

She tells the story in a city bar as a joke.
All the while she is shifting her life to become a circle.
She is signing up for courses to learn
the languages of meat and grass.

The Gaze

you can become an audience
to avoid the gaze

master the Greek chorus
to avoid the gaze

be safe rather than brave
to avoid the gaze

and still crave the gaze
for its burning

Box

When he knew what I loved
he bought me a desk in a flatpack box
and screwed it together for me.

I came home and a space had been made
for what I loved, a hard flat plane,
four legs and a drawer, a place for me
to write.

There are shapes you can make of love
without ever saying the word.

Baby, clarity is my core competency

The goal: a co-branded win-win.

Every day seems to bring a new kind of way to miss you.

By optimizing the value-add, brought to the table;

I held them in my throat but never spoke them.

building up a strong feedback loop;

To say them felt like offering something I couldn't retract.

facilitating actionable strategic integration,

Grab me by the chin,

strong liaising to utilize our shared platform;

let me inhale the taste of your breath,

applying metrics to the deliverables;

count your fingers on my back,

pro-actively leveraging alignment for competitive advantage;

shift my hips and arch.

fully optimizing the low hanging fruit;

Your weight …

and streamlining our best practice processes:

Your gaze ... I can't say it:

we will incentivize and empower true strategic synergy.

I love you.
I love you.
I love you.

Fact

for Stephen Cassidy

Lights and sound blink
like cage bars, drum *fun fun fun*
like a demand. That point in the night.

He takes my shoulders,
gaze freighted and earnest,
ready to impart a truth.

Honey, there's no *prize*
when you win a dance-off.
There's only *pride*
in a job well done.

Gravity

There is a way your joy pulls
when you smile at the floor, as we sit
separate and slide another bead
onto the string of conversation.
No, more like dust suspended in still water,
flecks of mica gold in the light that angles
through before it falls to sediment.
It was that kind of gradual accrual, and over it
the sun motes of your attention.
We talked until three on empathy and
words and TV and walked home
and separated awkwardly at the door.
There is a way your joy travels up
from the floor and into your face
that others reflect. Find it kindled.
Once, camping, I left the heavy pack
by the creek and walked the trail unladen,
feeling as though I was levitating over the roots
and stones. Being around you
feels like setting something down.

Thigh

thigh layered on thigh
a rising like strings
tugged stiff for tuning,
then strummed—
thumb on a bottom lip
breath
      like something ripping

Scanner

It is some knuckled punch beneath my ribs
that has me placing my palm on my chest
like I've been touched by a kind gesture.

As an adolescent girl, shy of new people,
I wrote in my diary, *How will they like me
if I don't know who they want me to be?*

I hug this grumbling tool the way I'd cling
to a lover I didn't want to leave. As a teen,
what I wouldn't have given for others
to have a machine to see into my heart.

I want it to unlock in me all that is uncertain;
my body not to be a thing which lies in wait.
The ache sits alongside my lungs, swelling
and contracting, my every sigh a relief.

And this paper gown flares and the scanner
clicks and reads and somehow all the lights
are too bright and the doctor used the word
'sinister' in a voicemail and then didn't answer.

Occasionally, I see it

From the northbound train to Drogheda
in a wink I saw a man riding a white horse
along the edge of the surf,
behind him the shallow bay and stretching sky.

Walking down Camden Street, I saw the butcher
with the lopsided wood block and Mad Hatter hair
standing behind his counter, rubbing his eyes,
elbows out and both fists swiveling, as a child might.

Standing at the door of my back garden in Harold's Cross
I heard my neighbour—whose face I wouldn't recognize—
speak to her daffodils like they were daughters.

Farm Visit in Clare

He stood in the muck of his family field
before the soar and knead
of gray Mullaghmore, in the silence
he fought to protect, and shouted
Hopkins' *The Windhover*, from memory,
at the wheeling hawk as it strode high
there on its steady air over his back pasture,
and he looked up as he belted the stanzas
and arched his back for the joy of it,
for our audience, for the mastery of the thing.

In his gnarled charisma he leads us through
the drainage, past the plantings as we tread
weak-ankled, wet and chattering to a holy well
furred with moss, waits as we array ourselves.
He plunges his hand in and pulls out
a heap of pound coins, winking in the mud.
Performing for the assembled group,
he pauses, nods to the solemn collared figure in the back,
gestures to the view that swallows us,
swinging wide away, and up. He says,
Apologies Father, but there's more than one way
you can buy a ticket to Heaven.

Drop Everything, Inis Oírr

In a certain rainless light
the whole island
turns tropical,
the air carbonated
with some conjured breeze—

an art-directed postcard:
doleful cartoon horse over a stacked wall
and blue-green sea,
a ceaseless, stretching day
threaded with effortless magic.

      The slow turning night.
      A jubilant crowd.
      The drop of the beat.

      I swallowed it all,
      warm music insinuating
      itself in me.

      Three hundred spines flexing
      and falling
      among the quiet stones and pastures.

      Some kind of exalted neon
      and wing, shine
      and chatter, faces
      alternating between sea and star,
      another song.

He lifted my hands as the music rose.

Keep throwing
your head back,
he said.

Late Night, Distant Sea

This wedding cake was a waste
of money, my mate says
back in daily life after the big event.
He hacked me off a slice and wrapped it.
Now the moon's pale glare
is pooling on the floor of this room
that smells of old dinner, my own small
chaos the only thing
rearranging the stifling air.
I leave it to sit on the stairs
before the oxygen rush
of the distant sea.
That second step
is rotting, I swear to God I'm going
to break my ankle some morning,
but just now, it's holding strong.
And I'm loving that waste
of money now, forked out of this
dry husk of foil,
the ganache stiff at the edges,
watching the moon's milky reflection
a wavering slick on the sea.
My breath in the cold is
a lid off a pot on the boil,
the steam rising into endless air.
It's easy to begin thinking
there's no one in the world
to witness this but me,
that everyone I ever gave my heart
needed me until they didn't,
that there's nothing moving

anywhere at all right now
except for the sea. And me—
sitting hunched against the cold
with a mouth full of sweetness,
and shivering—that moon,
and its reflection.

3

Meningitis

There's a low beeping,
some constant rhythm
everywhere no matter
what the hour of night.

I know that every ping
is the sound of a heart
succeeding but it is
the effect of metal scraping

on this raw mind.
Brightness
hurts my eyes.

I haven't
seen a hospital since they
first opened. This near-miss.
This inflamed reprisal.

I have veins that blow
and falter under the toxic
slide of medicine.

The flesh of my arm rises
and flushes around the needles
leaking cold fluid in an hourly fumbling.
Faces drag into positivity
for my benefit.

It's all in my head, I joke.
But my brain's swollen rind

twangs and I can feel my spine
all the way to my tailbone.

I don't have the energy
to be embarrassed
at my helplessness.

I marvel at all people will do
for me, what they will bring
how far they have come.

If I asked them for water
they'd lift my fragile head.

My mother in America
is looking for flights.

We Fall Asleep and Wake Each Time
to a Different World

She's convinced that the flights
age her, that they pressurize the water
of her cells, their swell and
dryness coarsening her,
the collective stale breath,
a mass exhale cycled through
to be breathed again.

She's convinced the flying's aged her,
not from anxiety;
she's accustomed to the sudden
bump and rumble, the constant
low jet moan. She doesn't even
lift her eyes when others
clutch armrests, superstitious
as ball players before a game.

Me, I believe in the gospel of statistics
but still I text my mom every time
I get on a plane.

She's convinced flying ages her,
but growing older is just a moving
from one place to the next, a trip
alone and heavy-laden.

The yellow disc of lake
catching the sun at evening
the scrape of human construction
in our net of grids and

lights, the secret of brightness,
the depth of cloud,
the rain under it,

all this faith,
all this giving up we do
to let whatever it is
that carries us, carry us on.

The Way I Sleep Now

It could be the skew of jet lag,
where a body can't catch up
to the technology that moves it.
I've flown back to find
it's already autumn here,
the corners of night pulled tighter in.
Or it could be the body asserting itself
in a foreign routine becoming
familiar, absent—the fear of going.
Before I left I'd spend half the night
pressing my face at different angles
into the pillow to find the one
that would tip me into darkness.
I'd list whatever lapse and shortcoming
may have bloomed into this punishment.
Since I've returned, I have a Masters in sleep,
the kind you have to rub off and creep from,
like I've met a man in an office
and made an arrangement for rest
that requires a journey in and out.

Throughout

for Kathy Kelly

Throughout the cellular blooming, the brine swell
and uplift, the suck and cry, the tumble;
throughout a thousand early risings;
throughout the crackle of identity, the self
in its bruising formation; throughout obstacles,
doubt and the bleak creature of insecurity,
too many options and not enough; throughout
the rain and the transatlantic flights; throughout a heart
raw with love, so broken it barely beat; throughout
funeral and split; packing boxes that burst;
throughout nights weeping, a soft palm upon
my hairline; throughout collapse and standing;
throughout push and path-finding; throughout—
I had the exquisite luck of a good mother.

Fallen Pines

The stand of pines in front of the house had to go.

They had done their job: drank light and grew.
They had a view of the sweeping ridges.
But their tall postures shaded the row of windows
fronting the house.

They all went with a cicada scream of chainsaws
and suddenly the house didn't know itself. It was
as though we were seeing it for the first time,
how in direct daylight you can see both the lines
on someone's face and the layered colours
of their eyes. The house was warmer then, and kept the heat.

I'd padded down among the fallen pines, cross-hatched
across the hill and found, at the side away from porches
and paths, a kind of cave made from trunks,
branches of green needles making walls and roof
like the folded wings of a bird. It was mine—the marvel
of a space not-there one day and now, there.

I would sit in the cave, heady at being alone, the power
of no one knowing. Peek out at the sky through the needles
like eyelashes. I carried Mason jars of well water and hid them,
kept a book on the shelf of an angled branch until, the next day,
I came to find its pages fluffy and waterlogged, the needles
beginning to fall with my every breath.

Crawdads

Curling rhododendron,
dappled sun like something discarded
on the leaves, jostling nettles.

Hushed water, a flow ripe from rain,
dim granite, soft swathes of Appalachian mud,
vines straining for sunlight.

Feet, moon-pale beneath the water,
hair dark as leaf-rot falling as he bends
to flip the broad stones, the right ones,
the muffled clunk and splash.

The swirling mud, the blind grasp,
lifted, all squirming points and hardness,
a dripping insect, claws and coiled life.

It shudders and scuttles its exoskeleton
on his soft palm. He turns it back
to the current, opening his hand in release.

Harvest

It's midnight
and there are twigs
cascading down among
giddy curses.
We're snatching pears
from an unruly tree
in front of a house
with boarded-up windows
and a beat-up pathway
caked with fruit.
Me and a boy
from the neighborhood
drawn to the harvest
wherever it rises.

There's nothing for the picking
up in Northwest,
with the fertilized lawns
and topiary.
On the train line
through Southeast DC
we troll a vacant lot
for exclamations
of mint and sage
from some long-gone
kitchen garden.

Down the train line,
I'm the only white girl
for a mile
and the disgraced ex-mayor

drives a Lexus
with a busted headlight
and bloodshot eyes
and plenty of soft-skinned things
fall to bruise and burst
on this pavement.

We enter a bar
smelling like some
exotic breeze.
A boy inside asks me
for weed,
but all I have
is handfuls of apples;
our bounty sprung
from somebody's
abandonment.

The Grainy Picture

Dark pool, puffs of flame
and blurring smoke:
all that is inflicted on all
we've agreed as enemy.

And yet despite
the regiment, the panic,
despite the coiled instinct
attuned to a single cry, sometimes
(sometimes!) lessons in killing
don't stick.

My own beloveds, the grainy pictures,
the ramrod stance, the stories
they don't tell. I hope for them
a secret in that chaos, a half-passive
rising, lifting ever so slightly
towards the horizon:

in the churn and bluster
of our own compounding mess
we sometimes (sometimes!) find
the divine lever which angles
our rifles towards the sky.

In the singular chaos
of the front, let us cling
to the blessing of men
missing on purpose.

Espero

from the Spanish esperar, 'to wish, to wait'

1

Night dark as a yawn as I arrive determined
to commit the crime of remaining.
How quickly the desert dried the water from the river.
How quickly the desert became my mouth.

2

Pick the lint from your T-shirt, *bebe*,
like the blankets I lift from the looms,
the factory air that turns to felt in my lungs.
Pick an eyelash from your cheek
and blow it away with a wish. Baby.

3

I held you in an airless back corner over five day's journey
for the indignities of this job—for your flawless English.
Your carpeted school. You can read the signs.
I can read the rumors in the smoking area.

4

In class my child learns the words for travel:
that is *car*, that is *bus*, that is *boat*, that one, *plane*.

The teacher points at the drawing of the 18-wheeler, the *truck*.
My child replies, "That one is *bumpy*."

5

I can stretch the span of your shoulder blades
with my hand as I kneel before you in our kitchen.
I choreographed this conversation all night: my nightmares
now a plan. There's word of *la redada*: the raid.

6

My children are effervescent with concern,
acutely independent: they know the number
on the fridge to call if they come home one day
and I don't. *Imigración* is a big word in small mouths.

7

From behind, people in handcuffs
look like they're praying, upside down.
Their small empires, built and gone
for a stamp on a form.

8

I lift my hands to cup the bulbs of your shoulders.
They socket in my palms. Milk sits on the counter.
How do I say: *Children, you are marked for your dreams now.*
How do I say: *I will find my way back.*

9

I send them on the school bus to wonder through every test
and lesson and song whether their home at the other end
of this longest day will be dark and still, without me.
Without me: not a home. They carry it like books in their bags.

10

Children: I walked through a desert humming with the deep
industry of loving you.
They should mark me, I think. I am stronger than they can
imagine, I think. The men arrive at the mill.
I think. I can't think. I think of you.

Conflict Resolution

"A strike as a result of a contract dispute within the catering service led to Baghdad-style looting in the cafeterias of the United Nations..."
— TIME, *April 2003*

The contract's up, and a middle manager's casual aside
informs a small army of single mothers and three-train
commuters that accumulated overtime isn't coming,
and, by the way, no pay for today. So, in a sudden
uprising of inaction the ladling palms stay still.

Everything's free across the glorious global cafeterias:
Belgian chocolates and oxtail soup, hard rolls,
the lunch time wines across the draped tablecloths.

Bodies queue through towered halls on 44th St, every sculpture
and splashed mural an allegory for peace, hands clutching
in racial balance. The rumor spreads. The diplomats begin to run.

The gentleman from Geneva grabs a box of baklava
from an intern as the gentleman from Hungary fills
his two-button blazer with stainless cutlery and the
gentleman from Canada hoards peanut M&Ms as the
gentleman from Laos ladles potatoes into plastic cups.

Cuff-linked wrists scrape trays of croissants into shopping bags,
heft cases of sparkling water and, unbound by etiquette,
muss continental hair shellacked with gel.
Desk drawers waft the steam of looted roast.

The gentleman from Geneva speaks gently
into his beige earpiece; he underlines the need
to facilitate the provision of humanitarian assistance

through the most effective channels; he calls for
a further maintenance of peace.

With regards to the incidents of the day, rest assured
he will issue a strongly worded condemnation.

Raleigh Central, 2 a.m.

Muttered bullhorn hymns, as if any melody
is a balm here, as if we could startle awake
the governor with another verse of *Amazing Grace.*
As the hymn rises, the thought will not leave me:
Will they even bother to disinfect his arm?

The MLK Boulevard roars over streets of small
mill houses, near enough to bounce a football off the fence.
This place must be hell on property values.

This place must be hell. His heart is a bird tethered
to his veins and flapping. We protect candles
against an enduring wind. He must be closing his eyes
against the bright fluorescents.

They must be fumbling at the soft crook of his elbow.

Songs waver and fall still. We are here to resist.
We are waiting for a heart to stop so we can go back home.
We are waiting. Our prayers are fumes, floating.

The guards explode from the doors, run to their cars,
pass us eyes ahead and pedal down: a whole shift
fleeing as though from the scene of a crime.

State policy mandates after working
an execution, you take the next morning off. They go home
to stand by the light of the fridge. A light softer than fluorescents.
Shutting their eyes against the cool.

I imagine them sleeping in. Lying awake.
I wonder why the fridge never actually smells of food.
There is another car that leaves last, and so slow.

4

The Fireman

He can be forgiven for the jolt
of exhilaration that still comes
from running traffic lights, as the world
pauses and parts for his swirling colours
and the parabola of his bawling siren.

He can be forgiven for that mild thrill.
He mentions as an aside most firemen die
before sixty, just around retirement, as though
it's safety that deflates them.

He can be forgiven for laughing too loud
on nights off at the pub with his mates.
His lungs have hauled the same cargo of
smoke as theirs. He's mastered, as they did,
the whiplash of sleep to practiced sprint.

He can be forgiven for keeping it light at lunch.
How can he explain that heat? How to listen
to the creak of the floor for discordant notes
of collapse? Anecdote the drape of families
on the pavement, faces lit by all they own?

He can be forgiven for refusing to elaborate
the infernos of his daily grind, for keeping
his witness to himself. Life at its fragile cracking;
a language in ashes, remedy too often too late.

Ink

He pulls them dripping
from the container
in a rain of brine,
their sea-sweat running
down his forearms,
their ink smudging
the matte bed of ice.
A drip of gray drizzle
melts around his feet.

He piles wet handfuls,
flattened as dropped gloves,
casings disheartened
with gravity.
They slip and glisten,
seem to shrink before the cold.
He rearranges them. Pauses.
Shifts them again.

Him, ink-stained to his elbows,
head bent to his daily task.
With blackened palms
he pours out all
the bucket contains.
He entreats to passersby
his message in ink:
Come and buy,
come and eat.

You store things up and you live on it

The succulents were everywhere,
and huge, set like mosaic pieces,
and I had never seen them grow wild
(in the ground!) like real plants.
They looked plastic: thick and waxed.
My grandfather kept one
on the windowsill,
by the kitchen sink,
and every two weeks
he put one ice cube
on the soil of the pot
and let it melt.
They store it up and live on it.
My aunt, from New Orleans,
who doesn't travel much
since the floods, comes all the way
to California. Upon arriving
among the blissed-out yogis,
she yells way too loud: *Will you just look at*
these fucking succulents, baby!
I've never seen them so big.

Seeing Jeremy See Snow

Try and recall the last time
you saw something
for the first time.

Displaced from Texas heat,
he'd wear four layers
and never get warm.
He'd cross his gym-built arms,
say he's *fucking fine* and blow
hot breath onto his fingers.

He'd lash contempt to everything
he said and I wondered what he'd fled
in dusty Texas.

He spent the autumn raging,
thought the winter was worth hating.
Then one time we asked him
a question, waited for the quick retort.
He was silent.

When we looked, he was wide-eyed,
staring right by us
to the window full of snow
as it fell thick and slow
for his very first time.

We opened a door to the curtain of it—
heavy, fragile, elegant.
We pulled him out
and saw him see it.

The slack muscle of wonder
slung his lips open, left him empty
of sullen replies.
He was silent as it sighed
down upon his upturned arms.

Try and recall the last thing
you saw for the first time.

To know something exists
but not the handful of its realness—
Jeremy,
I could explain snow
by whispering on your skin:
It's like this.

But you held your arms out
in the muffling stillness
and met it on your own.
Were you marked, even then,
for loss? Was that the absence
that we saw?

Or for a minute
with your arms out
were you marked instead
for awe?

Try and recall the last time
you saw something
for the first time.

Home from Home

Is it on me like a tattoo,
or in me like an accent?
Or is it just the first stop on a long route,
where I keep my toothbrush in the bathroom?

Is it on me like complexion?
Is it in me to the marrow?
Or is it just a bad Skype connection,
how my slang's inflected now?

Or maybe I love to feel a little bit exotic—
the chance to be whoever I want;
move over here and feel like an artist.
But to walk into a room with my whole life known:
There is more than one answer to the question of home.

Is it on me like an outfit,
or in me like a wish?
Or is it the end of a transatlantic flight
to where all my anecdotes live?

Is it on me like a label?
Is it in me like a habit?
Or is it when my mom says, *I think you're staying, baby*,
and in response to it I'm silent.

My old friends don't call much when they're upset,
but I don't call either.
I don't know my mom's routine,
I don't know what to tell my father.
And that Dublin damp might keep the Carolina dust down.

But home—my eyes well up at the smell of the ground.

Is home what I knew, or is home what I know?
And how do you know when to stay and when to go?

Is it on me like a burden?
Or is it in me like a kindness?
Is it on me like a yearning?
Is it in me like a conscience?
Is it on me like a posture?
Is it in me like confession?
Is it on me like an option?
Is it in me like a lesson?
How do you name that pull in your bones?
In three years I'll be gone longer
than I was ever home.

When Your Country is a Weapon

I've tried to explain to Americans
that the light is different here.
At home at the peak of summer
the sun sets at barely nine
but here, like a pitcher poured out
slow and fine, in practice and principle,
the evening is diluted by light.
I used to take pictures of the night
just to send to people. And then, at once,
it turns a corner and, like a switch,
suddenly it's dark.

The texts poured in, after the news.
I'm sorry; I'm so sorry, hun; I'm sorry.
And that one friend, who isn't politically active,
texts: *How the hell am I supposed to ignore him*
when he isn't calling me? I text back:
Are you watching what's on TV?
And to the rest, all I want to write is:
I'm so sorry. I'm sorry. I'm so so sorry.

It's winter, low clouds, and I'm turning off
the news when I can't stand it.
I wake up to frost on my bedroom window.
And what have we done, and I don't know,
and I find, beyond the hangover of an election night party
everyone left in silence, that I cannot leave bed
for a whole day because what have we done
and the ground is fuzzed with cold, and the swans
on the canal are picking at crispy frozen grass,
and what have we done and what have we done

and what has been done to us?
In Ireland, it's all pubs exhaling steam into the night
and now I watch the news like it's something
that bruises me. What we chose.
I can't be at another social justice meeting
if the focus isn't on how to reach those who'd never show.

I'm not from here, and no matter how long
I've been here, I'll not be from here.
It's been eight years almost—
the length of two presidential terms.
My friends back there are concerned. They text:
Do they hate us? What have we done?

What can you do when something ugly unfurls?
When your country is a weapon
that chops at the world? What do you do
when a bully knows he's been chosen?
And your heart is a weapon that throbs at the words?

You write, I guess. You sit
and start to make a plan.

I've tried to tell Americans
that the light is different here—
here the light stretches like it was poured
from a pitcher, water spreading across the tablecloth
until everything saturates—
that you can get drunk on light in July.

If the future's something we have to brace
ourselves against, can we find a space in the dark,
and lift courage from the mess?

Inhale a voiceless kindness, and hold the breath?
What are we doing? What have we done?
The evenings will stretch again
until half the night is gone.

August in New Orleans

for Susan and George

and it's hot as a breath,
town at the bottom of a bowl.
Shoulders of concrete press
against Lake Ponchartrain
and the curved legs of the levees
spoon the Mississippi.
A foolish place to make a place.

August in New Orleans
and the city is an old woman
up too late in a dress too young for her,
baptized in bourbon, watching
the weather roll in.
One deep low pressure system,
one perfect angle, and a lazy corps of engineers
drowned Canal St. and the shotgun houses
of citizens made refugees.

August in New Orleans
and my uncle jokes
his hurricane evacuation plan
 is *a canoe and a gun.* We laugh
until we see them leaning there
in the garage. My family
mixing strong Old Fashioneds
and tap-dancing a comedy routine.
But they're quick to anger,
can't sleep, refuse to travel.
They look at houses on steep hills.

It's August in New Orleans
and the river is pouring
from storm drains, spilling through
windows, and a higher floor
is a gift. Down in the Lower 9
they're clawing their way out of attics,
watching plaster slough off like skin,
sweat-washed on rooftops, waving
at helicopters that only hover.

August in New Orleans
and a framed newspaper photo of my uncle
standing before a wall of black mould,
holding just a spray bottle of bleach.
My aunt points out the window they jumped from,
their battery radio. They floated away
but drove back, to blue tarps for ruined roofs,
country-dark nights in the city centre,
watermarks on buildings high as men.

Salt and Iron

God as my witness:
these pixels cannot capture
a soul as it steams from concrete
among the sidewalk's glass dust.

God as my witness:
Jackson dipped his hands in blood and smeared them
down his white shirt
and wore it for three days stained.

God as my witness:
a mother mirrors her son's last posture
as though knees were made for collapse.

God as my witness:
we should dye our thread with every spattered blast;
we should not eat for tasting salt and iron;
we should mourn like mothers,
knees bruising as they hit the ground.

My Father, Skydiver

for Rick Fornoff

Tucked in his old ratty Ts that reached our knees,
we'd fall asleep to tales of flying.
Imagine a light head and heavy straps
and engine drone and wind.

Wrapped in flannel sheets, we'd shoulder folded nylon,
look out at a flat quilt of Texas ranches,
angle our wrists like rudders through the severe clear
of a blue day towards a bulldozed runway seeded with grass.

We'd dream of gravity, of the pull that startles small shapes
into fabric fireworks drifting like jellyfish on down.
(He swears the nerves leave you after thirty tries.)

The magic just a mastery of physics and drag—nylon,
folded, shouldered, and unfurled
until the people on the ground called him down
to fill our heads with news of the sky.

We all watch our fathers fall to earth.
They become less tall. No longer know it all.
5'10" and fallible, thinks I don't call enough—
but he's still the man who flew,

who bent to smooth sheets, brought reverence
to a whisper, said *Remember, so much depends on yes.*
So face the breath of wind, out-shout your frantic heart,
and leap with arms out wide.

Lightning Source UK Ltd.
Milton Keynes UK
UKHW012037190720
366822UK00003B/129